A Day Without Immigrants

Rallying Behind America's Newcomers

by Jeannine Ouellette

A Day Without Immigrants

Rallying Behind America's Newcomers

by Jeannine Ouellette

Content Adviser: Lisa Magaña, Ph.D., Associate Professor,
Transborder Chicano/a and Latino/a Studies,
Arizona State University

Reading Adviser: Rosemary G. Palmer, Ph.D., Department of Literacy,
College of Education, Boise State University

Compass Point Books ✦ Minneapolis, Minnesota

COMPASS POINT BOOKS

3109 West 50th Street, #115
Minneapolis, MN 55410

 This book was manufactured with paper containing
at least 10 percent post-consumer waste.

For Compass Point Books
Brenda Haugen, Jennifer VanVoorst, Jaime Martens,
Lori Bye, XNR Productions, Inc., Catherine Neitge,
Keith Griffin, Nick Healy

Editorial Direction: Red Line Editorial, Inc., Bob Temple
Editor: Patricia Stockland
Page Production: Lindaanne Donohoe

Library of Congress Cataloging-in-Publication Data
Ouellette, Jeannine.
  A day without immigrants : rallying behind America's newcomers /
by Jeannine Ouellette.
      p. cm. — (Snapshots in history)
  ISBN-13: 978-0-7565-2498-2 (library binding)
  ISBN-10: 0-7565-2498-9 (library binding)
 1. Migrant labor—United States—Juvenile literature.
 2. Immigrants—United States—Juvenile literature.
 3. Illegal aliens—United States—Juvenile literature.
 4. Emigration and immigration law—United States—Juvenile
literature. I. Title. II. Series.
  HD5856.U5O94 2008
  331.6'20973—dc22   2007004679

Visit Compass Point Books on the Internet at
www.compasspointbooks.com
or e-mail your request to
custserv@compasspointbooks.com

A DAY WITHOUT IMMIGRANTS

CONTENTS

Rallying to Be Heard

In the early hours of May 1, 2006, Carlos awoke. He scanned the peaceful morning sky from his apartment on the northern edge of Manhattan in New York City. Eight years earlier, Carlos and his wife and children had moved to the United States from Mexico. Carlos is one of more than 1 million immigrants who leave their home countries to settle in the United States each year.

As the sun rose on that first morning of May, Carlos heard the soft crackle of the radio filling his tiny kitchen. The announcer read the day's news in Spanish. It was Monday, a workday. Carlos grabbed a cup of coffee. In a few minutes, his foreman would pull up with the rest of the construction crew to head to the job site.

But this morning, Carlos would not be joining the crew. This morning would be different.

It was "A Day Without Immigrants." It was a day to join together with other immigrants and concerned people across the country to protest a bill that had passed five months earlier in the U.S. House of Representatives.

Representative James Sensenbrenner, a Republican congressman, had introduced the bill that Carlos and other immigrants were protesting. Sensenbrenner's bill called for increasing penalties on immigrants who enter the United States illegally. The bill also called for reducing the number of future immigrants allowed to enter the United States legally. This bill became known by its congressional code: H.R 4437. It sparked immediate anger and debate. Immigrants around the nation organized themselves to show

On May 1, 2006, demonstrators in Chicago, Illinois, and other cities throughout the United States gathered to show support for immigrant rights.

their strength and their disapproval of what they saw as unfair immigration law.

In Los Angeles, California, a city with one of the largest immigrant populations in the country, groups such as the Latino Movement USA, Hermandad Mexicana Nacional, and the Coalition for Humane Immigration Rights–Los Angeles responded quickly. They were soon joined by regional and national organizations, such as the League of United Latin American Citizens. More than 100 groups organized the first rally to protest the bill in Los Angeles on March 25, 2006. An estimated 500,000 people protested on that day. Other cities followed Los Angeles' lead and organized rallies of their own in the following days.

Meanwhile, organizers in Los Angeles came together to form the "March 25 Coalition." This group led the charge in calling for a nationwide protest of H.R. 4437. At first

WHO IS AN IMMIGRANT?

There are several types of immigrants:

Legal immigrants have gone through the governmental channels and paperwork to change their citizenship to American. They have the same rights as an American born citizen, except they can't become president or vice president. Legal immigrants are also called naturalized citizens.

Illegal immigrants live in a country other than their own, but they haven't been granted citizenship. Illegal immigrants are also called illegal aliens.

Refugees are people seeking asylum, or safety, from events happening in their home country. In the country they flee to, refugees may live as citizens under the protection of the government. However, they can only stay for a certain period of time.

they called their event "The Great American Boycott." They chose May 1 as the day it would take place. In many countries, May 1 is a special holiday for recognizing workers, as is September's Labor Day in the United States. It seemed fitting to hold the protest on this special day.

By holding a national protest, organizers wanted to send a message to the U.S. government and the country. They wanted to prove that its 35 million immigrants are vital to the American economy. They also wanted recognition and respect for people such as Carlos, who is one of the 9 million or more immigrants who live in the United States illegally. By protesting together on the same day in cities throughout the United States, many immigrants could raise their voices as one. On May 1, they were to stay home from work,

In Los Angeles, crowds filled the streets on A Day Without Immigrants.

11

rally, and march in their towns and cities. They also were to refrain from making any purchases. Actions such as these—if enough people participated—would show just how important immigrants are to the nation. If they stayed home, work would not get done. If they didn't buy anything, businesses would lose money. And if they joined together in the streets and showed their strength, the U.S. Congress might be convinced to change its policies.

In Carlos' kitchen, the radio announcer raised his voice. He called out, *"Un dia sin immigrantes!"* (A Day Without Immigrants!) Behind Carlos stood his wife and 13-year-old daughter. They were smiling. His wife would not go to work today, and their daughter was not going to school. All three of them were going to march in protest.

By midday, the small family stood together in Washington Square Park in lower Manhattan. They were surrounded by an estimated crowd of more than 200,000 people. Next to them were other

MAKING A BILL INTO A LAW

Congress, made up of the House of Representatives and the Senate, is responsible for writing laws that govern the United States. A member of Congress introduces a bill, and other members vote to pass the bill or reject it. If the bill is passed by both chambers (the House and Senate), it is sent to the president of the United States. The president then approves the bill and signs it or rejects the bill with a veto and requests Congress write a new version. Alternatively, if the president vetoes a bill, Congress can override that veto with a two-thirds majority vote. Once the president signs a bill, it becomes law.

Mexican workers. Some had traveled hundreds of miles to attend. There was a Senegalese busboy, a Chinese waiter, a nanny from Jamaica, and others representing numerous different nations. Many were illegal immigrants like Carlos.

"White Americans don't know what it's like to live every day without papers," Carlos told newspaper reporters. As an undocumented worker, Carlos did not give his last name for fear of being discovered and deported.

> *We've been working here eight years. We've been paying taxes. Our children are going to school. Now we have to pay more to send our other daughter to City College because we are not "residents." We have been applying for papers, but it's impossible. ... The only right we have is to work hard and not demand anything.*

Carlos turned back to the crowd, joining in the singing and chanting. He wanted to be part of this historic event.

More than 1 million people flooded the nation's streets to make their voices heard. Immigrants from all over the world joined forces to make A Day Without Immigrants one of the largest nationwide demonstrations in 30 years. Police in Chicago, Illinois, estimated that by late morning 300,000 people had gathered in that city's center. Across New York City, people formed human chains, some stretching for miles, and marched to Union Square. In Los Angeles, 200,000 people marched to City

13

Hall in the morning, and another 400,000 marched that evening. From Milwaukee, Wisconsin, to Miami, Florida, to Seattle, Washington, people rallied. One young mother, Melanie Lugo, protested with 50,000 others in Denver, Colorado. She told television reporters that immigrants, legal or illegal, are the backbone of what America is.

> *It doesn't matter. We butter each other's bread. They need us as much as we need them.*

But not all demonstrations were in support of the immigrant cause. In many cities, demonstrations in favor of H.R. 4437 took place. Though smaller in numbers, many participants spoke harshly against illegal immigrants. They wanted tougher restrictions. Retired Army Colonel Albert Rodriguez called for an appreciation of new citizens but not illegal residents. He said:

SUPPORTING A CAUSE

Organizations such as Latino Movement USA, Hermandad Mexicana Nacional, the Coalition for Humane Immigration Rights—Los Angeles, and the League of United Latin American Citizens are groups that fight for immigrant and refugee rights as well as equality for Hispanic citizens. They also represent migrant workers and labor unions.

> *We and millions of others like us did it legally. We're all here today to tell all those illegal protesters, "You do not speak for me."*

With thousands of workers staying off their jobs, many businesses were forced to close for the day. Some stores closed to show support for the immigrant cause. Other stores that stayed open reported no sales. In many school districts with high immigrant populations, parents kept their children home for the day. In San Francisco, more than 50,000 protesters shouted, "We are united!"

By nightfall, supporters had declared A Day Without Immigrants a major success. They called on Congress to vote against H.R. 4437. And they announced a campaign to register voters from among immigrants who had recently obtained citizenship.

That fall, many members of Congress were up for re-election. If enough voters disagreed with their congressperson's stance on immigration law, they could vote that person out of office. ◣

Chinatown in New York City witnessed demonstrators voicing their support for immigrants and their disagreement with the Border Reform bill.

Immigrant Nation

The United States is a nation of immigrants. Only American Indians are considered "native" to the country. But they, too, were once immigrants. More than 11,000 years ago, ancestors of today's American Indians trekked to North America from northern Asia. They walked to what is now Alaska and gradually drifted southward to settle throughout North America. All other Americans can trace their family histories to different nations around the globe.

When explorer Christopher Columbus sailed to North America in 1492, Europeans saw the land as a "New World" full of riches and opportunity. During the next 300 years, immigrants sailed across the ocean from Europe to what is now the United States.

Most came from Great Britain, which included England, Scotland, Wales, and for many years, Ireland. Others came from Germany, France, the Netherlands, and other European countries. Many Africans came by force as slaves.

Immigrants landed at Castle Garden in New York, the first official U.S. immigration center, before Ellis Island opened in 1892.

Immigrants set off to the New World for many reasons. Most imagined a better place to earn a living and raise families. Some fled war, disease, and poverty in their homelands. Others, such as the Pilgrims who founded Plymouth Colony in 1620, wanted religious freedom.

During the next century, Great Britain established 13 New World colonies on land between what is now New Hampshire and Georgia.

In 1776, America declared its independence from Britain. At that time, most of the people living in the colonies were of British descent.

In 1790, the United States passed its first naturalization law that ruled how an immigrant could become a citizen. The law said that only "free white persons" who had lived in the United States at least two years could become U.S. citizens. The law denied citizenship to Africans, Asians, indentured servants (people contracted to work for a set length of time for someone else), and most women.

Meanwhile, many people continued to seek fresh starts in America. At first, only a few thousand immigrants arrived each year. By 1820, immigration started to increase dramatically. A third of these newcomers were Irish immigrants fleeing hardship in their home country. The others were mostly German, British, and French.

THE WAVES OF IMMIGRANTS

In 1790, the United States held its first census. This official population count showed 3.9 million Americans. More than 2.5 million were from Britain, with the vast majority coming from England. Between 1831 and 1840, nearly 600,000 new immigrants streamed into the United States— a vast difference from the approximately 6,000 immigrants arriving each year in the late 1700s. By 1850, more than 780,000 Irish had moved to the United States. That same decade saw 780,000 new immigrants from Germany, England, and France. From 1850 to 1880, more than 220,000 Chinese immigrated to the United States. Between 1900 and 1910, nearly 129,000 Japanese men on temporary contracts arrived to work in Hawaii. From 1911 to 1929, more than 1 million Mexicans took refuge in the United States.

During the 1840s, a series of events drove throngs of people from all walks of life to America. The first event was a combination of war, bad harvests, and faltering economies across Europe. Nations in Europe were involved in civil wars as well as battles with each other. As crops failed from bad weather, disease, and war-torn fields, the economies in many nations suffered.

The Statue of Liberty was a welcome sight for many European newcomers after weeks of travel aboard ship.

The second event came in 1845 when one of the worst famines in history struck Ireland. The potato crop, Ireland's main source of food and income, was destroyed by drought and disease. The famine lasted four years. More than 1 million people starved to death. Hundreds of thousands more fled their homeland. By 1850, more than 780,000 Irish had moved to the United States and settled mostly in the Northeast. During the same decade, failed political revolutions in Europe brought another wave of immigrants from Germany, Great Britain, and France.

The third major event sent U.S. immigration skyrocketing. Gold was discovered in California. The great California Gold Rush sent people racing across the country. It also spurred a new wave of immigration from other nations. For the first time, large numbers of Asians arrived, mostly from China. From 1850 to 1880, Chinese workers immigrated to build the fast-growing railroads across the United States. Meanwhile, Mexicans headed north in search of gold. The U.S. victory at the end of the Mexican War in 1848 brought the promise of U.S. citizenship to more than 50,000 Mexicans living in newly acquired U.S. land in the West and the Southwest.

During the mid- to late 1800s, land in the United States was plentiful. To encourage movement westward, the government even offered free land in the Midwest and West. Many states granted white male immigrants the right to vote as soon as they

declared their intentions to become citizens. Not until the 14th Amendment in 1868 did the United States allow citizenship to African-Americans. By then, many African-American families had lived in the United States for generations. Women, regardless of race or citizenship, were not allowed to vote until the 19th Amendment was ratified in 1920.

The United States offered newcomers the chance for a better life. As the nation grew, so did immigration. Between 1880 and 1900, more than 2.5 million people arrived from Germany, Ireland, Great Britain, and Canada. At the turn of the century, greater numbers of immigrants came from

In 1882, a political cartoonist depicted racial stereotypes to make a point about the Chinese Exclusion Act. The blocks in the wall being built against the Chinese represent "prejudice," "fear," "jealousy," and "Un-American" ideas. The Chinese can be seen tearing down their own wall. This represents the open trade that China had approved during the same time.

countries such as Poland, Russia, Italy, Sweden, and Norway. More than 1 million Jewish immigrants fled oppression in Eastern Europe. The year 1907 set a new immigration record at Ellis Island in New York when approximately 1.25 million people entered the United States.

Some immigrants came but did not stay. In the early 1900s, hundreds of thousands of Mexicans flocked to the United States to escape a revolution in their country. But when the fighting died down, nearly half moved back to Mexico. At other times, immigrants who had planned to stay for a short time settled permanently. More than 100,000 Japanese men on temporary contracts arrived to work in Hawaii between 1900 and 1910. Some eventually returned to Japan, but many stayed and sent for their wives and children.

The U.S. Congress had passed the Chinese Exclusion Act in 1882. This law limited the number of Chinese allowed into the country each year. Several factors fueled the resistance to Chinese immigration. People from China did not look like Europeans, their language did not resemble English, and their customs and religious beliefs differed dramatically from people of European descent. Most Americans with European ancestry found Chinese culture and customs difficult to understand. They saw Chinese ways as strange, mysterious, and something to distrust.

Another factor was resistance from workers in the American West. These workers felt that the Chinese were taking jobs away from others and driving down everyone's wages in the process. The Chinese Exclusion Act of 1882 was one of the first significant restrictions to immigration. But it would not be the last. The factors behind it would appear again in the nation's history. And they would appear on May 1, 2006, A Day Without Immigrants. ◣

Reaching for a Dream

Chapter

3

The mass immigration that began in the 1880s continued for nearly 40 years, not slowing down until the United States entered World War I in 1917. Eighteen million new citizens arrived during those 40 years and changed the face of the nation forever.

Among the immigrants who arrived around the turn of the century was a young Jewish writer from England named Israel Zangwill. In 1908, Zangwill turned his own immigration story into a play called *The Melting Pot*. That title became a famous phrase to describe how the United States became home to millions of immigrants. In Zangwill's visions are those of many others— the United States as a great melting pot. People from all over the world jumped into the pot and transformed as they blended into

English playwright and novelist Israel Zangwill described the United States as a "melting pot," which has become a famous analogy of the nation's mixed population.

something much larger and new. To jump into Zangwill's melting pot meant leaving one's past behind, setting aside differences, and living together in harmony. Most of all, it meant "melting" into a shared new identity as Americans. Almost anyone could come to the United States. It was the land of opportunity. Even the poorest immigrant had a chance for a fresh start.

One of the first landmarks an immigrant like Israel Zangwill saw upon arriving in the United States was the Statue of Liberty. No other image

The Statue of Liberty overlooks Ellis Island, the immigration station that processed millions of immigrants into the United States.

is more closely connected to the U.S. immigrant experience. At the base of the statue is the poem *The New Colossus* by Emma Lazarus:

> *Give me your tired, your poor,*
> *Your huddled masses yearning to breathe free,*
> *The wretched refuse of your teeming shore.*
> *Send these, the homeless, tempest-tost to me,*
> *I lift my lamp beside the golden door!*

Near the Statue of Liberty is Ellis Island. During its years of operation, from 1892 to 1954, the immigration station at Ellis Island ushered 12 million immigrants into the United States. Steamers anchored in the New York harbor, and arriving passengers rode in small ferryboats to reach the island. They were led into an enormous brick building to begin the process of legally entering the United States. They climbed a long flight of stairs. At the top, teams of doctors waited to identify people who had contagious diseases or might be too weak to work. These immigrants could be sent back to their ships and returned to their homelands. Medical rejection happened to about 2 percent of the people entering Ellis Island. But most people passed the medical exam and moved on to the Great Hall to begin registration.

The Great Hall was a vast room where thousands of immigrants waited in line to meet an inspector. The inspector recorded an immigrant's name and country of origin and examined identification papers to make sure everything was accurate. For most immigrants, registration was a simple process. About five hours later, weary travelers exited the doors at the other end of the building and rode on ferries to New York or New Jersey to begin their new lives in America.

Ellis Island was the nation's busiest entry point. It processed thousands of immigrant arrivals each day, and it set a record on April 17, 1907, when 11,747 immigrants passed through its gates.

Today almost half of all United States citizens can trace their family histories back to Ellis Island.

But immigrants also arrived at many other ports, from Maine to New Orleans. Millions arrived on the West Coast, too, especially in San Francisco Bay at a place called Angel Island.

Angel Island opened in 1910, and unlike Ellis Island, it was designed to keep people out. It became know as "The Guardian of the Western Gate." Many immigrants arriving in San Francisco were Chinese. The Chinese Exclusion Act of 1882 was in effect, so only a small number of Chinese immigrants who arrived at Angel Island were allowed into the United States. Some waited on the island for months or years to be processed. Angel Island also received and rejected other Asians from Japan and the Philippines.

Ellis Island and Angel Island were two very different places. Ellis Island was seen as friendly and welcoming. Angel Island was more restrictive and

WHAT IS A VISA?

A visa is a document the U.S. government gives to a foreign citizen to enter the country. There were no visas used during the immigration boom in the late 1880s and early 1900s. Today, however, many kinds of visas are used depending on the reason the immigrant wishes to enter the country. There are visas for students, foreign government officials, business visitors, athletes, travelers, temporary workers, personal employees, medical personnel, entertainers, children, and much more. How long a person needs to stay in the country and the reason they're traveling to the country help determine which type of visa they receive.

closed to immigration. These two images illustrate the range of attitudes toward immigration after the 1880s.

As more immigrants poured into the United States, many Americans didn't like how the face of the nation was changing. They wanted more limits and restrictions.

By the early 1900s, the United States had a long history of immigration from Northern

Angel Island was not as welcoming as Ellis Island. Many Asian immigrants waited months, or even years, in internment barracks before being processed or sent home.

29

In 1908, Little Italy in New York City was one of many ethnically-centered neighborhoods in which new immigrants settled.

Europe, mostly England, Ireland, and Germany. Some Americans believed that the United States was founded on this unique heritage. They believed that the laws, culture, and people should forever reflect this ethnic group. They did not want immigrants from other countries, even from Eastern and Southern Europe, to change their culture.

But the doors had been open a long time. By 1910, millions of immigrants from nations such as Poland, Russia, and Italy had arrived. They clustered into neighborhoods centered on their ethnic heritage. In large cities, each ethnic neighborhood was like a tiny country bordered by roads and sidewalks. Businesses catered to the customs and preferences of the residents. Places such as Chinatown and Little Italy in New York City resulted from new immigrants establishing their own ethnic neighborhoods. But separate neighborhoods could cause misunderstandings and distrust between different groups of people.

Religion could also be a trouble spot. Religious freedom was a basic right in the United States from its beginning. However, the majority of Americans were Protestant Christians, and many of them resisted the arrival of others who held different beliefs. From 1880 to 1917, more than 1 million Jews came to the United States, and even more Catholics poured in from Ireland, Italy, Poland, and the rest of Eastern Europe.

In the early 1900s, calls for restrictions on immigration rang out. American workers argued against cheap labor. They said immigrants would take jobs away from American citizens and push down wages. Nativism was strong. American-born citizens did not want immigrants entering the country. The Chinese Exclusion Act represented a strong negative attitude toward Asians in general. This exclusion act was supposed to last 10 years.

During its peak years, Ellis Island saw thousands of immigrants pass through every day.

Then the Geary Act extended it for another 10 years. In 1902, Congress renewed the law with no end date. It was not repealed until 1943. Even then, the law allowed for only 105 Chinese immigrants per year. That's a tiny number compared to the thousands of immigrants who passed through Ellis Island in a single day.

Xenophobia, or fear and hatred toward foreigners, also was strong. Many Americans wanted the

United States to stay isolated from other countries. They did not want to get involved in World War I (1914–1918). They wanted the United States to separate itself from the problems of the world. Many Americans feared war, economic hardship, disease, and people with different ideas about government. To many Americans, the world outside the United States seemed like a threatening place. Now, suddenly, immigrants representing those threats stepped onto American soil.

In 1917, the government was pressured to act. First, it imposed a literacy requirement. In order to enter the United States, an immigrant over the age of 16 must read and write in his native language. Not many immigrants could do that because education in their home countries was not readily available, especially for the poor. The goal was to keep out people who might not be able to find work.

The 1917 changes to the Chinese Exclusion Act closed doors to immigrants from nearly all of East Asia and the Pacific Islands. More limitations were imposed with the Emergency Quota Act in 1921. For the first time, restrictions were placed on immigration from the Eastern Hemisphere, including Europe, Africa, and the nations in Asia not already included in the Chinese Exclusion Act. For each country, only a specific number of people would be allowed to enter the United States each year. Just 3 percent of the number of immigrants who had arrived from that country in 1910 would be allowed to come to the United States each year.

A country such as Germany, with high immigration in 1910, would be allowed a large number of immigrants in 1921. But a country such as Poland, with fewer immigrants in 1910, would be allowed a small number of immigrants under the new rule. The quota rule ensured that immigrant groups from Germany, England, and Ireland would stay ahead of others. Also, the law did not set limits on highly trained workers, such as doctors, accountants, and skilled craftspeople. This allowed even more German, British, and Irish immigrants to enter if they were skilled laborers.

In 1924, the rule allowed immigration numbers to become even more lopsided. New quotas would be based on 2 percent of each country's immigration numbers from 1890. The immigration gap with Northern Europeans grew larger. Still, some Americans wanted greater isolation. Senator Ellison DuRant Smith, of South Carolina, said:

> *The time has arrived when we should shut the door. ... Thank God we have in America perhaps the largest percentage of any country in the world of the pure, unadulterated Anglo-Saxon stock. ... It is for the preservation of that splendid stock that has characterized us that I would make this ... a country to assimilate and perfect that splendid type of manhood.*

The quota system, however, was not imposed on immigrants from Mexico and Central and South America. Their numbers were low, and

farms and ranches in the Southwest welcomed the cheap labor.

The quota system of 1924 became the main tool to control immigration for decades to come. Between World War I and World War II, immigration to the United States almost stopped. During the Great Depression (1929–1939), when millions of Americans were out of work, the government further

Refugees from Russia came to the United States during World War I.

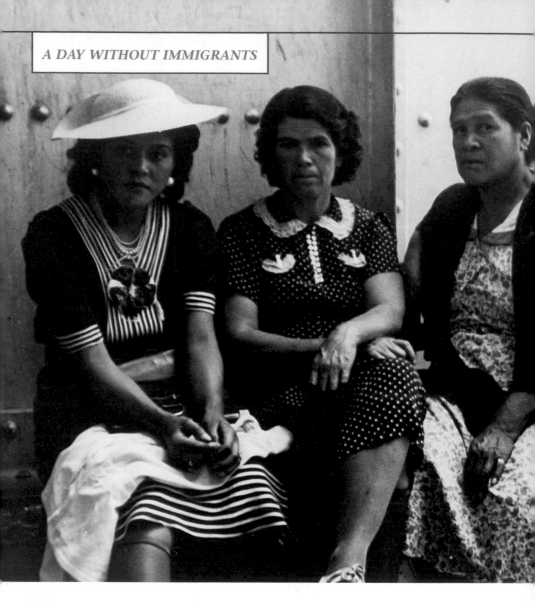

The bracero program allowed Mexican workers to enter the United States during World War II.

restricted immigration and only allowed a few thousand newcomers, mostly Europeans, to enter the country. Other immigrants were repatriated, or forced to return to their home countries. More than half a million people, most of Mexican descent, were sent back to Mexico. But in August 1942, the repatriation ended with the start of the bracero program. The United States' participation in World War II created the need for workers. The

Under the bracero program, the Mexican government was promised that the braceros would earn $1.40 per hour. The contracts allowed the braceros to stay in the United States for extended periods. Farmworkers already living and toiling in the fields were paid much less. The difference in pay led farmworkers who weren't part of the bracero program to strike. During this time, the braceros did an extensive amount of agricultural labor. Often the workers faced harassment and discrimination. When they returned to their home country, the braceros had trouble finding work. Many had been financially exploited by their U.S. employers as well as shunned by people in Mexico. The program ended in 1964.

bracero program allowed skilled farm laborers from Mexico to enter the country. They were needed to help sustain U.S. agriculture during the war. Then, after World War II ended in 1945, European war refugees sought safety in the United States. In 1948, the quotas were temporarily lifted, and more than 600,000 immigrants arrived in the United States.

During the 1950s, the United States entered another period of restraint and xenophobia. The Soviet Union, a powerful communist nation, was seen as a threat and a rival for world power. The United States kept immigration low, except for political refugees fleeing Soviet control. In 1952, immigration was limited to 175,455 people a year.

In 1954, about 80,000 illegal immigrants were expelled from the United States. Most of these people were from Mexico. They had lived and worked in the United States for years under the bracero program.

In the 1960s, attitudes in the United States about race and ethnic heritage slowly shifted toward greater acceptance. In 1965, the Hart-Cellar Act ended the quota system. Under the new law, immigration was based on family sponsorship. Preference was given to immigrants with family members already in the United States. That family member could apply to "sponsor" a relative to come to the United States. Another change in the law included limiting immigration from the Western Hemisphere (Canada, Mexico, and Central and South America) to 120,000 people a year. Immigration from the Eastern Hemisphere was limited to 170,000 people. The limitations did not apply to skilled workers,

DAILY ENTRY

Every day, approximately 600,000 foreigners are processed through U.S. Customs and Border Protection. This figure includes tourists as well as immigrants arriving with some form of extended-stay visa. There are 317 official entry points.

ESTIMATED IMMIGRATION TOTALS IN THE UNITED STATES

Years	Estimated Number of Immigrants
1821–1830	143,439
1831–1840	599,125
1841–1850	1,713,251
1851–1860	2,589,214
1861–1870	2,314,824
1871–1880	2,812,191
1881–1890	5,246,613
1891–1900	3,687,564
1901–1910	8,795,386
1911–1920	5,735,811
1921–1930	4,107,209
1931–1940	528,431
1941–1950	1,035,039
1951–1960	2,515,479
1961–1970	3,321,677
1971–1980	4,493,314
1981–1990	7,338,062
1991–2000	9,095,417
2001	1,064,318
2002	1,063,732
2003	705,827
2004	957,883
2005	1,122,373

Very low numbers in some decades reflect the effects of different immigration laws, restrictions, or social climates during that time period.

and thousands were allowed to enter the United States each year. In addition, extra openings were made for thousands of refugees fleeing war and escaping from communist countries.

The changes in immigration law brought a steady increase in the number of people allowed into the United States. For the first time, large numbers arrived from Asia, Africa, Central and South America, and Mexico. The United States was on the threshold of a new immigration boom.

39

The Modern Immigration Boom

Chapter

4

Immigration in the United States has soared from 4.5 million new immigrants in the 1970s to 9 million in the 1990s. In 2005, legal immigration to the United States totaled 1.12 million. For the first time in U.S. history, major groups of immigrants no longer came from Europe.

From 1981 to 1990, Mexican immigration totaled more than 1.5 million people—more than triple the immigration total of any other nation. In the next 10 years, Mexican immigration increased to more than 2 million. The explosion of immigration from Mexico and other nations to the south of the United States has several causes.

One major factor is family sponsorship. A single immigrant might come to the United States, find a job, and begin the process of sponsoring his family. Visas might be approved for his wife and three children. A few years later, he might obtain visas for his brother and sister, who in turn sponsor their own families.

There also are important economic factors. Mexico and most countries in Central and South America are known as developing nations with economies that are small and still growing. Money is scarce, jobs are hard to find, and unemployment is high. People come to the United States to seek better lives. Many workers send part of their income to family back home. Often the money an immigrant sends home is much more than family members can earn in a developing country. Poverty and unemployment are factors that push a person away from his or her homeland.

Green cards allow immigrants to stay permanently in the United States.

One of the strongest factors pulling people to the United States is jobs. Many U.S. industries welcome immigrant workers. These companies pay low wages, and most Americans won't take the jobs. Many immigrants without professional skills or knowledge of English take unskilled jobs in factories, agriculture, hotels, and restaurants. Employers argue that they need to pay low wages to keep costs down, and many immigrants are willing to do low-paying work because they have few other options.

Another factor behind U.S. immigration is location. The United States and Mexico share a land border from California to Texas, making the United States easier to reach than other parts of the world. In less than a day, a Mexican immigrant can take an inexpensive bus ride to a border entry point, such as El Paso, Texas. A Guatemalan or Salvadoran might make a similar inexpensive journey in less than two days. In comparison, it costs thousands of dollars for an immigrant from Kenya to take a plane across the Atlantic Ocean.

War has been another factor. During the 1970s and 1980s, Guatemala, Nicaragua, and El Salvador suffered civil wars. Guatemala's struggle continued for 36 years (1960–1996). Death, destruction of homes, and the resulting chaos and poverty forced hundreds of thousands to flee. In the 1980s, more than 200,000 Salvadorans came to the United States. Another 215,000 followed in the 1990s.

Despite the restrictions, quota systems, and resistance, no other country has ever been as open to immigration as the United States. No other nation is made up of so many people from different backgrounds. Today more than 35 million immigrants live in the United States. Immigrants make up 12.4 percent of the 300 million people living in the United States. That percentage is nearly as high as it was during the boom of immigration in 1910 when 14.8 percent of U.S. residents were immigrants. This modern immigration boom is again changing the face of the nation. Immigrants have affected the U.S. economy and culture. New neighborhoods, businesses, and cultural organizations have sprung up to offer goods and services where none existed 10 years ago.

Some immigrants find work with construction companies and are willing to take lower pay for unskilled tasks.

The biggest change has been the rapid growth of the Hispanic population. Hispanics passed African-Americans as the second largest U.S. ethnic group (after whites of European descent) in 2005. According to July 2005 estimates, 14 percent of the U.S. population is Hispanic. African-Americans total 13.4 percent.

Whites of European descent are the minority population in cities such as Miami, San Antonio and El Paso, Texas, and Santa Ana, California. Los Angeles County has the largest Hispanic population at 4.2 million. New York City follows with almost 2.2 million, and the Chicago region has 1.4 million.

Immigrants work in all industries, including professional fields, business, agriculture, and labor. Some come to the United States to attend colleges and earn degrees, and many will stay and join the workforce with specialized skills. Many immigrants are doctors, computer programmers, accountants, and architects. But most immigrants work in unskilled, low-wage fields. One out of every five low-wage workers is

WESTERN HEMISPHERE IMMIGRATION

From 1980 to 2001, immigrants from Central American countries such as El Salvador, Guatemala, and Nicaragua and nations in South America totaled more than 2 million. Nearly 2 million more immigrants came from the Caribbean nations of Cuba, the Dominican Republic, Haiti, and others. Between 1991 and 2000, large groups came from the Philippines, China, India, and Africa. The largest growth came from Mexico, Central and South America, and the Caribbean.

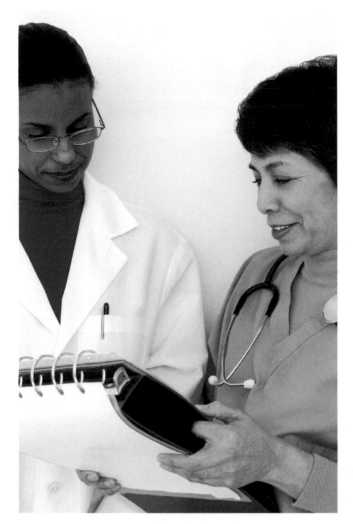

Immigrants work in professional fields such as health care and other skilled industries.

an immigrant. Most often they work in agriculture, fishing, and forestry. Hundreds of thousands of immigrants work on farms, picking fruits and vegetables for market. They travel from one field to the next to find work. Other immigrants clean homes and work as janitors for businesses and institutions. They also work in manufacturing, restaurants, hotels, construction, clerical services, and repair shops.

45

A DAY WITHOUT IMMIGRANTS

Immigrating while still in school may mean learning a new language in addition to new subjects.

Many immigrants come to the United States with little schooling. Almost one in five has less than a ninth-grade education. Young immigrants have a difficult time, too. They learn their school subjects and a new language at the same time.

As a result, 30 percent of all student immigrants drop out of high school. Many immigrants, however, learn to become part of the American culture by attending school. Public and private schools teach language and other subjects, as well as social rules. Sociologists refer to this type of environment as a "salad bowl" where people with different backgrounds learn to coexist, or to live among one another peacefully. A school classroom may include children from Russia, Mexico, China, and other nations. Each of these children may be learning English. Each comes to school with different cultural values and beliefs. But school can offer a common ground where English serves as the group language and where students are asked to share ideas, listen to others, and adopt rules of social behavior. Schools are like little salad bowls, mixing many different people.

Today's immigration boom has become a topic of serious debate. Some say immigration is good for the nation. Immigrants are often willing to do jobs no one else will do. They offer new talent and diverse ideas. And as they add to the demand for goods and services, more jobs are created as businesses hire more workers to meet these needs.

Others believe that immigration has become a problem. Their arguments are similar to those of 100 years ago. Immigrants take jobs away from Americans and bring their problems with them. They also believe that immigrants strain the nation's resources, including health care and schools.

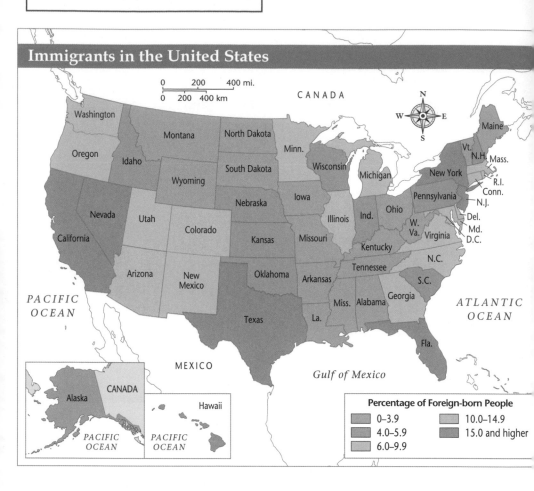

Immigrants in the United States

The percentage of foreign-born People

- 0–3.9
- 4.0–5.9
- 6.0–9.9
- 10.0–14.9
- 15.0 and higher

The percentage of foreign-born people living in each state in 2005 ranged from less than 4 percent to more than 15 percent.

Some think the United States will soon become a nation in which one group speaks English and another group speaks Spanish. Some argue that immigrants who cannot speak English and pass a language test shouldn't be allowed into the country. Others believe the United States should keep its Northern European heritage. They don't welcome the influences of Hispanics, Asians, and Africans.

There are also concerns about people coming to the United States who might deliberately harm the nation. The events of September 11, 2001, when terrorists hijacked airplanes and flew them into the World Trade Center in New York and the Pentagon in Washington, D.C., brought out many fears of future terrorist attacks. In the first two years after the September 11 tragedy, public opinion polls showed that most Americans wanted to decrease the number of new immigrants.

But one issue stands above all other concerns today. It's an issue that sparks more emotion and heated debate than any other immigration topic. That hotly debated issue is the problem of illegal immigration. Everyone recognizes the problem, but few agree on how to solve it. ◣

Crossing Borders:
Illegal Immigration

Chapter
5

The most common kind of illegal immigrant is one who remains longer than his or her visa allows. Foreigners must get visas, even to stay a short time in the United States. About half of "undocumented" immigrants arrive in the United States legally. They have visas that allow them to stay for a limited time. Eventually, the visa expires, or runs out. But the visitor stays with a family member or friend and gets settled into a job. These illegal immigrants, or "overstayers," may live in the United States for months or years before their expired paperwork is discovered by immigration officials.

The other kind of illegal immigrant is a person who slips across the border. These are the people shown on the TV news. They get caught hiding in the back of a truck at a California entry point

or in a ship in the New York harbor, or they swim across the Rio Grande into Texas. Some make dangerous trips by foot across the border. Miguel Penate is a manager in a fast-food restaurant in Phoenix, Arizona. He illegally immigrated to the United States from El Salvador in 1999. He said he had no choice.

Two Mexican men assess a piece of the fence along California's border. Illegally crossing the border has been a dangerous journey for many.

There's no way to come legally over here. If there was, do you think people would like to be in the desert risking their lives?

51

The Immigration Reform and Control Act of 1986 was supposed to reduce illegal immigration. But since the 1990s, illegal immigration has skyrocketed. Today the average number of illegal immigrants entering the country each year is nearly the same as legal immigrants, approximately 750,000. That has never happened before in U.S. history.

Illegal immigrants come for the same reasons legal immigrants do. They want jobs and better lives. Often driven by severe poverty, illegal immigrants are too desperate to wait many months for a visa.

Few people want to live in the United States as illegal immigrants and spend their lives in hiding. Their job options are limited, and they often work as day laborers, which is illegal. Day laborers gather on street corners early in the morning, waiting to be hired for one day of work, usually in construction or other manual jobs. Life goes on this way with no certainty of the next day's wages.

Illegal immigrants avoid doctors for fear of being caught. Each day holds the fear of being discovered, arrested by immigration officers, and deported back to their home countries.

Illegal immigrants are more likely to live in poverty than legal immigrants. It is estimated that two out of every five low-wage immigrant workers are illegal. If caught, employers face stiff fines for hiring undocumented workers, but in many industries such as agriculture and factory labor, the

rules are mostly ignored. About one in 20 workers is an illegal immigrant. That's nearly 5 percent of the total U.S. workforce.

Illegal day laborers risk discovery, arrest, and deportation for the hope of finding a day's work.

Some people believe that illegal immigration is useful. Low-wage workers help keep costs down, which means everyone pays less for food, products, and services. They argue that most immigrants deserve the chance to apply for citizenship. Others believe illegal immigrants should be forced to leave the United States. They believe the costs of illegal immigration are higher than the benefits. They point out that undocumented workers are able to send their children to U.S. schools and receive free or low-cost medical treatment. Critics of illegal immigration claim that most illegal workers do not pay income taxes on their wages. Some receive government benefits through fraud, but those services come at a high cost to taxpayers. Those opposed to immigration also say that legal workers are seeing their wages forced down by the competition brought by undocumented workers.

Both sides of the issue argue passionately. But most economists show that in the end, illegal immigrants have only a small impact on the economy, partly positive and partly negative. Wages

A Raid on Illegal Immigrants Empties a Small Town

On September 1, 2006, a quiet morning in Stillmore, Georgia, turned into a frenzy when federal agents raided a local trailer park. They were searching for illegal immigrants. After a few hours, more than 120 people were arrested. Hundreds more fled into forests around the trailer park. Of the 1,000 residents in Stillmore, 900 work at the Crider poultry plant. When the plant was investigated a few months earlier, federal agents indentified more than 700 suspected illegal immigrants.

On the day of the raid, 2-year-old Victor Perez-Lopez was left behind with a family friend. His mother, an illegal immigrant, fled the trailer park. His father had already been deported to Mexico. But Victor was born in the United States and was therefore a legal citizen. Many deported people have to face the same question as Victor's parents did: Will their child be better off alone and a legal U.S. citizen, or with his family in a poor country?

are lower because of illegal immigration, but this is only for those workers in the very lowest paying jobs. The wages of professionals and middle-income workers are not affected by illegal immigrants.

Changes to laws have severely cut back the benefits an illegal immigrant can receive. Government aid such as food stamps, medical coverage, and income

Legal or illegal, immigrant children are allowed to attend public schools.

The immigration debate has been the forefront for years. In 2003, Representative Nancy Pelosi of California met with Mexico's then president, Vincente Fox, to discuss immigration law reform.

benefits are no longer available. But emergency medical aid and public education, two expensive services, are still available to undocumented workers and their families.

As for income taxes, many businesses withhold tax from illegal workers' pay. That tax is paid to the government as part of the company's total tax bill. As much as $7 billion a year gets collected from undocumented workers in just Social Security tax. But those same workers are not eligible to receive the benefits paid for by their taxes. Illegal immigrants also pay sales taxes, which are added to purchased goods. Immigration supporters

WHERE DO ILLEGAL IMMIGRANTS LIVE?

More than two-thirds of illegal immigrants live in eight states: California, Texas, Florida, New York, Arizona, Illinois, New Jersey, and North Carolina. One in six illegal immigrants is under the age of 18. A number of states rely heavily on undocumented workers.

Below are estimates of undocumented populations for each state.

Alabama 30,000–50,000	Idaho 25,000–45,000	Montana Less than 10,000	Rhode Island 20,000–40,000
Alaska Less than 10,000	Illinois 375,000–425,000	Nebraska 35,000–55,000	South Carolina 35,000–75,000
Arkansas 30,000–50,000	Indiana 55,000–85,000	New Hampshire 10,000–30,000	South Dakota Less than 10,000
Arizona 400,000–450,000	Kansas 40,000–70,000	New Jersey 350,000–425,000	Tennessee 100,000–150,000
California 2.5 million– 2.75 million	Kentucky 30,000–60,000	New Mexico 50,000–75,000	Texas 1.4 million– 1.6 million
Colorado 225,000–275,000	Louisiana 25,000–45,000	New York 550,000–650,000	Utah 75,000–100,000
Connecticut 70,000–100,000	Massachusetts 150,000–250,000	Nevada 150,000–200,000	Virginia 250,000–300,000
Washington, D.C. 15,000–30,000	Maryland 225,000–275,000	North Carolina 300,000–400,000	Vermont Less than 10,000
Delaware 15,000–35,000	Maine Less than 10,000	North Dakota Less than 10,000	Washington 200,000–250,000
Florida 800,000–950,000	Michigan 100,000–150,000	Ohio 75,000–150,000	Wisconsin 75,000–115,000
Georgia 350,000–450,000	Minnesota 75,000–100,000	Oklahoma 50,000–75,000	West Virginia Less than 10,000
Hawaii 20,000–35,000	Missouri 35,000–65,000	Oregon 125,000–175,000	Wyoming Less than 10,000
Iowa 55,000–85,000	Mississippi 30,000–50,000	Pennsylvania 125,000–175,000	

point to these payments as ways that undocumented workers are helping the economy. Finally, illegal immigrants do buy goods and services. This helps to generate business and jobs. ◣

The Raging Debate

The nearly 2,000-mile (3,200-kilometer) border between the United States and Mexico stretches from California to the Gulf of Mexico in Texas. Along this expansive border, an average of 8,200 illegal immigrants cross into the United States every day.

In April 2005, two men decided to take action to prevent illegal border crossings. Chris Simcox and James Gilchrist called on citizens to search for illegal immigrants. Simcox and Gilchrist named their group the Minutemen after the volunteer soldiers in the American Revolution who were willing to be called to battle at a moment's notice. Simcox and Gilchrist asked volunteers to arm themselves, take up positions along the Mexican border, and report illegal crossings to the U.S. Border Patrol. They argued that the U.S.

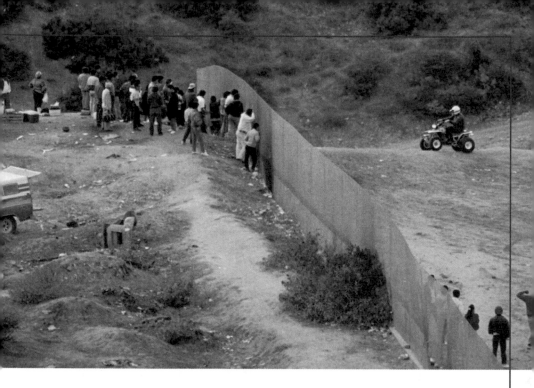

government was not doing enough to keep illegal immigrants out. The Minutemen wanted to attract attention to illegal border crossings. Their actions made news all across the United States and in other countries, especially Mexico.

Near San Diego, California, the border is closely watched by U.S. Border Patrol agents who are concerned about drug trafficking.

On April 5, 2005, the Minutemen reported their first sightings, and 18 illegal immigrants were arrested and deported.

The Minutemen drew strong reactions from all sides. Some called the Minutemen defenders of the country. A number of politicians supported their efforts. Don Goldwater, a Republican candidate for governor of Arizona, said he would build a "tent city" to hold illegal immigrants. Then he would use their labor to build a wall along the border. California Governor Arnold Schwarzenegger, an immigrant himself, claimed he would welcome the Minutemen to patrol his state's border.

A visa documents when a person has legally entered a foreign country and shows how long he or she can stay.

Others felt differently. Some expressed frustration that the group was taking the law into its own hands. Officials of U.S. Customs and Border Protection said that the Minutemen were getting involved where they did not belong. President George W. Bush spoke against them. He said:

> I'm against vigilantes in the United States of America. I'm for enforcing the law in a rational way.

The biggest reaction came from immigrants and organizations that support immigration, as well as people who sympathized with the plight of legal and illegal immigrants. "The Minuteman project has created a powder-keg situation with the potential to go beyond harassment and false imprisonment to real violence," said Eleanor Eisenberg, executive director of the American Civil Liberties Union of Arizona. The Minutemen have been accused of being racist, violent, and dangerous. Despite their unconventional and questionable methods, by the end of April 2005, the Minutemen counted 857 volunteers among their ranks.

Immigration supporters wanted to simplify the visa application process and make it easier for immigrants to follow a legal route. Supporters also believed that some illegal immigrants already living in the United States should be granted amnesty, or forgiveness for breaking the law. They should be allowed to apply for green cards without fear of being arrested and sent back to their home countries. This would put them on the path to becoming productive, tax-paying citizens.

THE NATIONAL GRAPE BOYCOTT

On September 8, 1965, farmworkers went on strike in Delano, California, to protest their low wages and poor working conditions on the grape farms. The workers also wanted social justice and to gain the respect of the nation for which they were working. Cesar Chavez and other labor union leaders joined the cause in nonviolent protest. The National Grape Boycott was the first of many migrant labor strikes and protests against the powerful grape farm owners.

61

Others believed U.S. immigration had gone too far. They wanted the border walls and more Border Patrol agents. They wanted increased law enforcement to track down illegal immigrants. Some also called for restricting legal immigration.

The arguments grew more heated. Both sides demanded official action. But nothing would happen unless the government created new laws or changed the way current laws were enforced.

The issue was a smoldering fire just waiting for the next spark. That spark came on December 6, 2005, when James Sensenbrenner, a member of the House of Representatives from Wisconsin, introduced the "Border Protection, Anti-Terrorism, and Illegal Immigration Control Act." Also called H.R. 4437, the bill was simple and direct. It would:

- Make being an illegal immigrant a felony and impose prison sentences for any illegal immigrant who was not immediately deported.

- Make it a felony to assist an illegal immigrant to enter the United States.

- Build a two-layer fence along 700 miles (1,120 km) of the U.S.-Mexican border.

- Require any non-Mexican illegal immigrant to be jailed before deportation processing.

- Increase employer fines for hiring undocumented workers: $7,500 for the

first offense, $15,000 for the second, and $40,000 for each one after that.

The H.R. 4437 bill significantly increases the amount of border protection, including additional border agents, especially in the Southwest.

- Cut off any pathway to legal status for an illegal immigrant no matter how long the immigrant had lived in the country

- Force illegal immigrants, if discovered, to immediately leave the United States. They could then apply for visas from outside the country. If granted visas, they could return legally.

- Limit legal immigration to what Congress considers a manageable level that benefits the economic, social, and cultural well-being of the United States.

63

In Washington, D.C., H.R. 4437 was passed by the House of Representatives on December 16, 2005. The bill then moved to the Senate.

Immigration supporters called Sensenbrenner's plan harsh and unforgiving. They said his ideas would make the situation worse. Most moderates—those whose views lie in the middle ground of an issue—also opposed the bill. Moderates said the bill offered no chance for illegal immigrants to stay in the country and apply for legal residence. President Bush did not agree with the bill. He supported a visiting worker program instead. He wanted illegal immigrants to have a chance to apply for legal status. Bush said:

> *We're not going to be able to deport people who have been here, working hard and raising their families. So I want to work with Congress to come up with a rational way forward.*

Anti-immigration groups supported the bill as the first step toward bringing both legal and illegal immigration under control.

The House of Representatives did not debate the bill for long. After only a few days, it passed by a vote of 239 to 182. The vote was along party lines, with most Republicans favoring the bill and most Democrats opposing it. Now the bill was ready to move on to the Senate.

Groups who support immigration encouraged citizens to speak out against the bill. They wanted the Senate to vote it down.

Many immigrant organizations worked together and urged supporters to call their senators and speak out for immigrant rights. Each group contacted people it served and distributed information on H.R. 4437. News about the bill was plastered on the Internet and TV and radio talk shows. Telemundo and Univision were among the numerous Spanish-language television networks that covered the issue on a daily basis. One popular radio personality, Eduardo Sotelo, worked hard to spread the word. His radio program was heard on Spanish-language radio stations across the country. "I'm one of them," he said. Sotelo was among the most influential individuals involved in organizing against H.R. 4437 and in the mass protests that followed.

On February 14, 2006, one of the first protests erupted in Philadelphia, Pennsylvania. Restaurant workers would have a one-day walk-out.

On March 10, 2006, thousands gathered in downtown Chicago to protest against the Border Reform bill.

66

They would stay home from work to show how valuable they were to employers and communities. February 14, Valentine's Day, is one of the most popular days of the year for eating in restaurants. Instead of going to work, the workers rallied at Independence Hall, where the Declaration of Independence was signed. Fewer than 2,000 protesters attended the event, but they drew nationwide media attention.

A few weeks later, several more groups banded together, this time in Chicago. Local Spanish-language radio stations and neighborhood churches helped get the word out. On the morning of March 10, about 100,000 people gathered in the city center and marched to the Federal Plaza in the heart of downtown.

Most of the demonstrators left their jobs for the day as an act of protest. Alex Garcia and 10 co-workers walked off their jobs at a sign company in a nearby suburb. He said:

> *Most people don't realize how much work we do, but it's part of their daily lives. We are putting up all the buildings and cooking all the food. Today, they'll understand.*

Around him the crowd chanted, *"Si se pueda."* (Yes, you can.)

EDUARDO SOTELO

Disc jockey Eduardo Sotelo illegally immigrated to the United States from Mexico in 1986 at the age of 16. He made the journey in the trunk of a car and crossed the border on foot. "I thought I was going to die in that car. I was in there for four hours," he said. Today Sotelo, who became a legal citizen in 1996, is one of the most popular Spanish-language disc jockeys in the United States. Sotelo used his radio program to advertise *Un Dia Sin Immigrantes,* and he urged other Spanish-language disc jockeys to do the same. He and the others who helped him are credited for bringing out huge crowds for the protests. "I told God that if he gave me an opportunity as a radio announcer, I was going to help my people," Sotelo said. "I think we have to make sure the message went through to Washington, to let them know we're not criminals."

67

Many important officials attended the rally. Chicago Mayor Richard M. Daley, Illinois Governor Rod Blagojevich, and Senator Richard Durbin were there. Representative Luis Gutierrez, of Chicago, spoke to the crowd. He said:

> *I have never been prouder to march, to show my commitment to a cause, than I have been today. We have brought together the true fabric of what Chicago is, of what our country is.*

The demonstration in Chicago touched off a flurry of activity in other cities. On March 23, about 15,000 people turned out in Milwaukee. A day later, 20,000 people rallied in Phoenix. In Los Angeles, organizers were also busy planning a rally of their own for March 25. As the date approached, local Spanish-language television and radio personalities got involved. Other popular disc jockeys joined Eduardo Sotelo in spreading the news. They encouraged people to turn out for the upcoming protest.

U.S. CITIES THAT DEMONSTRATED

Major cities that witnessed immigration law protests throughout the spring of 2006 included Detroit, San Diego, Minneapolis-St. Paul, Boston, Atlanta, Washington, D.C., Philadelphia, Phoenix, and Indianapolis.

When the day arrived, even rally organizers were surprised by the turnout of more than 500,000 people. The protest became known as *La Grande Marcha* (The Grand March). The gigantic march disrupted traffic in downtown Los Angeles for hours.

Marchers paraded through the streets shoulder to shoulder. Many wore white "peace" T-shirts. It was one of the largest demonstrations in Los Angeles' history.

The demonstrations in Chicago and Los Angeles spurred more organizing across the country. People protested in demonstrations from coast to coast, through the Midwest, North, and South.

Demonstrators held signs in a show of support.

Throughout April, protests continued. The enthusiasm shook politicians and anti-immigration groups alike. The Federation for American Immigration Reform condemned the rallies. Dan Stein, president of the anti-immigration group, expressed frustration:

> *Americans are outraged. These are people here illegally who are demanding rights that millions of hard-working, law-abiding Americans have fought to preserve. It is an insult to legal immigrants who are going through the proper channels legally and waiting in line for what is a right not a privilege.*

Meanwhile, local immigration leaders began forming a nationwide network. They wanted to plan a unified day of protest in every corner of the country, so they put out the announcement:

> *This movement's next action will be "The Great American Boycott 2006" on May 1. It will be a nationwide day without an immigrant, when immigrants and their supporters stay home from work and school, and businesses are closed.*

Many groups and networks responded quickly. By mid-April, more than 200 organizations had declared support for the national day of protest.

Again, calls to action came from the Spanish-language media. Every day, Sotelo and fellow disc jockeys around the country reminded listeners about

Protestors gathered near a day laborer sign on A Day Without Immigrants to send a message: Do not go to work. They wanted Americans to feel the impact of immigrant labor on the economy.

the boycott. They encouraged people to turn out for the marches. They also urged immigrants to show their appreciation for their new home by carrying the U.S. flag. Again and again, they announced *"Un dia sin immigrantes"* (A Day Without Immigrants).

71

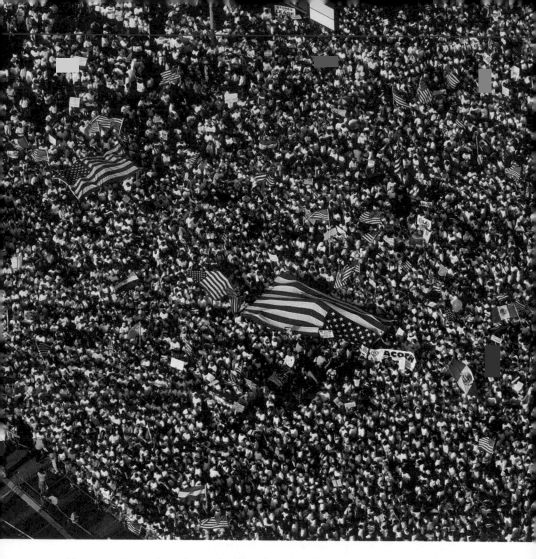

Legal and illegal immigrants were urged to stay away from their jobs for the day. If enough employees did not work, restaurants would close, construction sites would shut down, and many jobs would not get done for one day. Supporters were to stay out of stores to slow business to a standstill. And everyone was asked to join together and demonstrate against H.R. 4437. The hope was to show the power of large numbers of immigrants.

That power would be shown by people like Carlos and his family. When dawn arrived on May 1, people were already gathering in the streets. In New York City, they held hands and formed human chains to protest building a wall along the U.S.-Mexican border. By midday, more than 12,000 protesters marched over bridges and gathered in the heart of the city. They marched through Chinatown and Little Italy. They marched to Union Square and joined more than 200,000 people gathered there.

Demonstrations occurred in most major U.S. cities. In Miami, protesters marched through downtown and gathered at the Orange Bowl football stadium. Jose Cruz, a legal temporary worker from El Salvador, spoke out and said:

> *If I lose my job, it's worth it. It's worth losing my job several times to get my papers.*

More than 500,000 people turned out in Chicago. They filled the streets and brought traffic to a standstill. It was the largest protest in the city's history. In Milwaukee, 70,000 people protested. Milwaukee is close to the home district of H.R. 4377 author James Sensenbrenner.

The biggest event was in Los Angeles, where two protests occurred that day. The first came in the morning, with 300,000 people marching downtown. Another began in the afternoon, when 400,000 people marched. The parades lasted several hours and stretched for miles. Thousands of students attended A Day Without Immigrants rallies. The Los Angeles Unified School District reported more than

71,000 students in grades six through 12 absent that day. Los Angeles Mayor Antonio Villaraigosa announced:

> *These people out here want to be a part of the American dream. I support them.*

Disc jockey Eduardo Sotelo stood before cheering crowds, urging demonstrators to become citizens. An undocumented house cleaner from Mexico held up a sign that read, "We just want a taste of the American Dream." A 23-year-old restaurant worker said:

> *In my studies, I learned that there were demonstrations like this in Los Angeles during the Vietnam War. So it gives me chills to be part of it. Thirty years from now I'll look back and say, "I was there."*

Throughout the city, businesses closed or cut their hours for the day. The Seventh Street produce market closed for the protest, and vendors refused to fill orders for restaurants that depended on the market. Elsewhere in the country, many businesses also cut back. Tyson Foods closed five of its nine beef plants and four of its six pork plants. Cargill Meat Solutions gave 15,000 workers the day off to participate in rallies. Smithfield Foods used Monday to help workers write letters to their senators and representatives about immigration law reform. The Port of Los Angeles, the nation's largest shipping

facility, was almost completely shut down for the day. Nearly 90 percent of truckers did not report for deliveries.

A Day Without Immigrants created a sense of power and responsibility. Alejandra Arcasi, a naturalized citizen from Peru, marched before Los Angeles' City Hall. She said:

> Today we feel victorious. But still there is a lot more to do. ◣

Businesses and stores around the nation closed to support demonstrations for A Day Without Immigrants.

The Struggle Continues

Chapter

7

When night descended on May 1, 2006, nearly 1.5 million people had poured into the streets on behalf of America's immigrant community. Organizers believed the day caught the attention of the American people, and they hoped the protests inspired respect for legal and illegal immigrants. Chung-Wha Hong, executive director of the New York Immigration Coalition, said:

> *This will symbolize the interdependence of all of us, not just immigrants, but all of society.*

Opponents argued that the protests soured more Americans against immigration. Both sides hoped to make immigration a topic for voters in future elections. Every seat in the House of

Representatives and a third of all Senate seats would be up for election in six months. News organizations took opinion polls after May 1, and most of the polls showed that Americans showed greater goodwill toward immigrants. They saw the immigration issue in terms of three major questions: what to do about illegal immigrants living in the United States, how to handle new illegal immigrants, and how many legal immigrants should be allowed into the country in the future.

Many protesters waved American flags to show the importance of immigrants to the United States.

77

Days after A Day Without Immigrants, a CBS/*New York Times* opinion poll showed that 64 percent of Americans favored allowing illegal immigrants who lived and worked in the United States for at least two years to stay and apply for citizenship. That same week, a FOX News poll showed 68 percent of Americans in favor of allowing illegal immigrants with jobs to stay. After A Day Without Immigrants, Americans seemed more supportive of immigration overall.

Still, the public expressed concern about controlling illegal immigration. People favored stronger borders that would keep illegal immigrants out. In a CBS News poll, two-thirds of Americans said they wanted National Guard troops to patrol the U.S.-Mexican border. That same day, a FOX News poll showed that nearly eight out of 10 Americans favored more federal Border Patrol agents.

On A Day Without Immigrants, many immigrant groups wanted to voice their opinions by registering millions of immigrant citizens to vote. A favorite chant during the protests was *Ahora marchamos, mañana votamos.* (Today we march, tomorrow we vote.)

The chant was meant as a clear sign for politicians to take the protesters seriously. During the protest, volunteers helped people fill out voter registration cards and explained the voting process.

Some of the protest organizers formed the "We Are America Alliance" to get more people to vote in the

fall. They planned to work with churches, unions, and community centers to set up "immigrant action justice centers" to provide voter information and registration forms.

Ofelia Luna from Mexico became a U.S. citizen five years ago. But she had never registered to vote. After A Day Without Immigrants, she decided to register to vote in the 2008 presidential election. "I am part of this. I want my voice to be heard," she said.

Protesters wanted to remind Congress that the votes of the nation would be heard just as loudly as the chants of the marches.

The debate heated up in the House and Senate. The Senate worked hard to complete an alternative bill to H.R. 4437. After several slight changes, Senate bill S.2611 passed on May 25 by a vote of 62 to 36.

The Senate bill was considered much friendlier to immigrants than the House bill. The Senate bill would:

- Allow illegal immigrants who had lived in the country for five or more years to apply for green cards to become legal permanent residents.

- Increase the number of green cards from 140,000 a year to 650,000.

- Permit 200,000 additional guest-worker visas. This would give a person without a green card more time to apply for one while still working in the United States.

- Create a program allowing 1.5 million migrant workers a chance to gain legal residency.

At the same time, the Senate bill took a tough stance against new illegal immigration. It provided for 6,000 National Guard troops and the hiring of 3,000 Border Patrol agents to work on the U.S.-Mexican border. It also authorized 370 miles (592 km) of new fencing there. The Senate bill also surprised many on both sides declaring English as the country's national language. In more than 200 years, there had never been a national language. Immigrants groups were strongly offended.

VERBODEN TOEGANG
NO ADMITTANCE
ENTREE INTERDITE
EINGANG VERBOTEN
ART. 461 W. v. S.
ART. 88 9 A.R.P.

President Bush supported the Senate bill, which was much like his own proposal. He called S.2611 a good compromise. But a major problem still lay ahead. The House of Representatives had one bill, and the Senate had a different one. If an immigration reform bill were going to become law, both sides would have to agree on a single version.

Existing fences on the U.S.-Mexican border post warnings to those who might cross illegally.

If there was any hope of passing an immigration bill, it was going to take compromise. Politicians knew that the issue was making voters angry.

Immigration had quickly become a hot button issue. Whatever solution they came up with, one group or another was going to be unhappy about it. That unhappiness could mean lost votes.

Congressman Sensenbrenner was still leading the charge in the House. He angrily responded to both the Senate and the president. Of President Bush he said:

> *He basically turned his back on provisions of the House-passed bill, a lot of which we were requested to be put in the bill by the White House. That was last fall when we were drafting the bill, and now the president appears not to be interested in it at all.*

Sensenbrenner blasted the Senate bill, too. He said:

> *It is amnesty because it gives someone who broke the law the same rights as someone who obeyed it. We should not let lawbreakers jump the line.*

Reaching the necessary agreement to pass an immigration bill was going to take a lot of work. By autumn 2006, there was still no compromise in sight. Instead, the arguing in Congress had gotten worse. Outside of Washington, both immigration supporters and anti-immigration groups kept active. They were working to keep the issue in the spotlight and the pressure on Congress. The We are America Coalition and other immigrant rights groups continued their citizenship and voter registration campaigns. Along the border, the Minutemen staged new watches. Jim Gilchrist announced boldly:

> *The president could solve this problem tomorrow with an executive order and the Minutemen could go home. But until he does, we'll be here.*

And in every state, congressional election debates were under way. Immigration was often a part of the discussion.

By mid-September, with only seven weeks left before the elections, Congress had still not agreed on either the House or the Senate bill. Instead, politicians began picking out single rules from each bill. Then they passed the smaller sections as proposals on their own. Still, no agreements were reached between the two chambers of Congress.

Then, at the end of September, the Senate voted to approve a 700-mile (1,120-km) fence along the U.S.-Mexican border, the same length as the one agreed on in a House bill passed a few days before.

BUILDING A WALL

The 700-mile (1,120-km), double-layer wall approved by Congress would be constructed in several different sections along the U.S.-Mexican border. Each of the four border states would have sections built. The longest section would stretch from Calexico, California, to Douglas, Arizona, almost the entire length along the Arizona border. Another section would cover most of the New Mexico border and part of west Texas. The proposed wall would include radar, surveillance cameras, motion detectors, and unmanned aerial probes. The total cost is estimated at $6 billion.

83

The fence vote was taken as a severe blow by immigrant rights groups. It looked like a sign that Congress was going down a very restrictive path. Immigration groups vowed to make their voices heard on Election Day. Anti-immigration groups claimed it was the beginning of the sorts of changes the Minutemen had called for.

A DAY WITHOUT IMMIGRANTS ONE YEAR LATER

May 1, 2007, marked the one-year anniversary of A Day Without Immigrants. The ongoing debate over the House and Senate bills lessened the crowds compared to the previous year. But the tens of thousands of protesters who did demonstrate reminded voters that the issue was still unresolved.

But neither side could claim victory. A wall was not going to fix the problem on its own, especially not a wall that would leave 1,300 miles (2,100 km) of border wide open. On Election Day in November 2006, many Republicans lost their seats in Congress to Democrats. Some saw this as a sign that the nation wanted less restrictive immigration reforms. The people had spoken through their votes. But the immigration argument was not going away anytime soon.

The future of immigration reform remains uncertain. But, meanwhile, more than 8,000 illegal immigrants will continue to arrive in the United States every day for the foreseeable future.

Even if all of the illegal immigration stopped tomorrow, the face of the nation will continue

to change. The boom of Hispanic and Asian immigration during the last 30 years has already had an impact. It will continue to make an impression for decades to come. Census experts project that by 2050, nearly 25 percent of the U.S. population, or one in four people, will be of Hispanic descent. Currently, the population is 14 percent Hispanic.

Immigrants, legal and illegal, continue to come to the United States with the hope of finding a better life.

This new diversity can be found in cities and towns all across the United States. It's visible on the street, in schools and churches, and in the media. New immigrant voices are now part of the American experience, just like those of the Italians and Poles, the Germans and the Irish, and countless others who came before. As evidenced by A Day Without Immigrants, whether a harmonious melting pot or a salad bowl of mixed backgrounds, the United States is a nation of immigrants.

Timeline

1540

Spanish establish first European settlement of St. Augustine in what is now Florida

1607

First English settlement, located in what is now Jamestown, Virginia; first African slaves brought to Jamestown colony in 1619

1620

English Pilgrims settle Plymouth

1699

French settle Louisiana and Mississippi areas

1775–1783

American Revolutionary War

1790

First U.S. Census taken; U.S. total population counted at 3,929,214; 1790 Naturalization Act

1803

Louisiana Territory purchased from the French government

1830

First estimates of immigration from 1821–1830: 143,439

1845–1849

Irish potato famine

1848

Discovery of gold in California; beginning of the Gold Rush

1869

Transcontinental railroad completed

1882

Chinese Exclusion Act

1892

Ellis Island opens

1917

Immigration Act of 1917 (Asiatic Barred Zone Act)

1921

Emergency Quota Act

1924

National Origins Act of 1924 (Johnson-Reed Act)

1929–1939

Great Depression

August 4, 1942

The bracero program officially begins between the United States and Mexico

1952

Immigration and Nationality Act (McCarren-Walter Act)

1953

Refugee Relief Act

1964

Bracero program ends

September 6, 1965

Migrant farmworkers strike against grape growers in the National Grape Boycott in an effort to receive fair pay and better working conditions

1965

Immigration and Naturalization Services Act of 1965 (Hart-Cellar Act)

1980–1989

Illegal immigration totals 2.2 million

1986

Immigration Reform and Control Act (Simpson-Mazzoli Act)

1996

Illegal Immigration Reform and Immigrant Responsibility Act

1990–1999

Illegal immigration totals 5.2 million

September 11, 2001

Terrorist hijackers fly planes into the World Trade Center in New York City, destroying both buildings, and the Pentagon in Washington, D.C.

2000–2005

Illegal immigration totals 3.1 million

April 2005

James Gilchrist forms the Minutemen group to report illegal border crossings

February 14, 2006

Restaurant workers in Philadelphia, Pennsylvania, walk out as part of a protest for fair pay and immigration rights

Timeline

December 6, 2005

Representative James Sensenbrenner introduces bill H.R. 4437, the Border Protection, Antiterrorism, and Illegal Immigration Control Act

December 16, 2005

H.R. 4437 passes the House of Representatives with a vote of 239 to 182; the bill moves to the Senate

March 25, 2006

Crowds of half a million people gather in Los Angeles, Califonia, in The Grand March to protest against H.R. 4437

April 2006

Planning begins for the Great American Boycott 2006

May 1, 2006

A Day Without Immigrants sweeps the United States, with rallies,

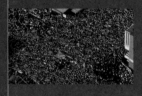 protests, and human chains forming in major cities throughout the nation

May 25, 2006

S.2611, the Senate's alternative to H.R. 4437, passes with a vote of 62 to 36

September 14, 2006

House approves a 700-mile (1,120-km) border fence as part of the larger immigrant reform bill

September 26, 2006

House and Senate negotiators agree to include $1.2 billion for fences and other border barriers in 2007 planning

September 29, 2006

Senate approves the border fence

November 7, 2006

Election Day results in many Republican losses and Democratic gains in both the House and Senate

ON THE WEB

For more information on this topic, use FactHound.

1 Go to www.facthound.com

2 Type in this book ID: 0756524989

3 Click on the *Fetch It* button. FactHound will find the
best Web sites for you.

HISTORIC SITES

Ellis Island Immigration Museum
National Park Service, Statue of Liberty National Monument and Ellis Island
New York, NY 10004
212/363-3200
Visitors can tour the grounds, the Main Hall, and read lists of names to see
who passed through the island's processing depot.

Angel Island State Park
P.O. Box 866
Tiburon, CA 94920
415/435-3522
Visitors can hike the island's terrain, take a guided tour of its historic sites,
and view the North Garrison barracks.

LOOK FOR ALL THE BOOKS IN THIS SERIES

The Berlin Wall:
Barrier to Freedom

Black Tuesday:
Prelude to the Depression

Third Parties:
Influential Political Alternatives

Freedom Rides:
Campaign for Equality

The March on Washington:
Uniting Against Racism

The National Grape Boycott:
A Victory for Farmworkers

The Teapot Dome Scandal:
Corruption Rocks 1920s America

A complete list of **Snapshots in History** titles is available on
our Web site: *www.compasspointbooks.com*

Glossary

amnesty
an official pardon or forgiveness for breaking a law

asylum
shelter or protection granted to a refugee

bracero
Spanish for "farmworker," also meaning a Mexican agricultural laborer working in the United States for a restricted period of time

campaign
organized actions and events toward a specific goal, such as being elected

emigrate
to leave a home country to settle in another country permanently

famine
an extreme shortage of food

felony
a serious crime, usually punishable by imprisonment

green card
a permit allowing a foreign person to live and work permanently in the United States

illegal alien
a person who does not have official permission to be living or working in the United States

immigrate
to come to live permanently in a foreign country

migrant
a person who moves to a new area or country, generally in search of work

racist
prejudice or discrimination against a person or group of a different race based on negative beliefs about that race

reform
to make or bring about social or political changes

refugee
a person who has had to leave a place to escape war or other disasters

visa
a permit that lets the holder enter and leave a foreign country and indicates how long he or she can stay in that country

U.S. Border Patrol
the official government officers who are trained to patrol and protect the U.S. border

Source Notes

Chapter 1:

Page 13, line 11: Sarah Ferguson. "A Day Without White People." *The Village Voice.* 2 May 2006, p.1. 16 August 2006. www.villagevoice.com/news/0618,ferguson,73086,2.html

Page 14, line 9: "A Day Without Immigrants." Foxnews.com. 1 May 2006. 16 August 2006. www.foxnews.com/story/0,2933,193761,00.html

Page 14, line 25: Ibid.

Chapter 3:

Page 34, line 20: Ellison DuRant Smith. Untitled speech. United States. 68th Congress. *Congressional Record.* 9 April 1924. Washington, D.C.: GPO, 1924, Vol. 65, pp. 5961–5962. 26 Aug. 2006. http://historymatters.gmu.edu/d/5080/

Chapter 5:

Page 51, line 8: "Tens of Thousands Rally for Immigrant Right." MSNBC.com. 10 April 2006. 16 August 2006. www.msnbc.msn.com/id/12250356/

Page 57, sidebar: "State by State Illegal Immigrants." NOW. 8 May 2007. www.pbs.org/now/politics/219/populations.html

Chapter 6:

Page 60, line 7: James G. Lake. "Bush Decries Border Project." *The Washington Times.* 24 March 2005. 1 Sept. 2006. www.washingtontimes.com/national/20050324-122200-6209r.htm

Page 61, line 6: Arthur H. Rotstein. "Minutemen Gather to Press Border Control." Breitbart.com. 1 April 2006. 14 August 2006. www.breitbart.com/news/2006/04/01/D8GNIHD00.html

Page 64, line 12: United States. White House. "President Bush discusses Immigration in Alexandria, Virginia." Office of the Press Secretary. 5 July 2006. 30 August 2006. www.whitehouse.gov/news/releases/2006/07/20060705.html

Page 65, line 24: Mandalit del Barco. "Spanish-Language DJ turns out the Crowds in L.A." *Morning Edition.* NPR.org. 12 April 2006. 15 August 2006. www.npr.org/templates/story/story.php?storyId=5337941

Page 67, line 23: Oscar Avila and Antonio Olivo. "Thousands march to Loop for Immigrants rights." *Chicago Tribune.* 11 March 2006, p. A1.

Page 67, sidebar: Mandalit del Barco. "Spanish-Language DJ turns out the Crowds in L.A." *Morning Edition.* NPR.org. 12 April 2006. 15 August 2006. www.npr.org/templates/story/story.php?storyId=5337941

Page 68, line 6: Ibid.

SOURCE NOTES

Page 70, line 7: Federation for American Immigration Reform (FAIR). "Monday Protests by Illegal Immigrants Expected to Add Fire to Heated Immigration Debate." 10 April 2006. 2 Sept. 2006. www.fairus.org/site/PageServer?pagena me=media_release4102006

Page 70, line 18: March 25 Coalition. "March 25 Coalition Statement." April 2006. 16 August 2006. www.arab-american.net/pdffiles/March_25_ Coalition_ Statement_as_of_4_4_06%5B1%5D.pdf

Page 73, line 14: "'A Day Without Immigrants.'" Foxnews.com. 1 May 2006. 16 August 2006. www.foxnews.com/story/0,2933,193761,00.html

Page 74, line 4: Anna Gorman, Marjorie Miller, and Mitchell Landsberg. "Marchers Fill L.A.'s Streets: Immigrants Demonstrate Peaceful Power." *Los Angeles Times.* 2 May 2006, p. A12.

Page 74, line 12: Ibid., p. A14.

Page 75, line 8: Ibid., p. A12.

Chapter 7:

Page 76, line 10: "'A Day Without Immigrants.'" Foxnews.com. 1 May 2006. 16 August 2006. www.foxnews.com/story/0,2933,193761,00.html

Page 79, line 9: Teresa Watanabe and Nicole Gaouette. "Next: Converting the Energy of Protest to Political Clout." *Los Angeles Times.* 2 May 2006, p. A1.

Page 82, line 9: Eric J. Frommer. "Sensenbrenner: Bush Turned Back on Bill." CBSNews.com. 17 May 2006. 15 August 2006. www.cbsnews.com/ stories/2006/05/17/ap/politics/mainD8HLRDR00.shtml

Page 82, line 17: Ibid.

Page 83, line 5: Stephanie Innes. "Battle at the Border." *Arizona Daily Star.* 29 Sept. 2006. 30 Sept. 2006. www.azstarnet.com/sn/rionuevo/146868

SELECT BIBLIOGRAPHY

Andreas, Peter, and Thomas J. Bierstaker. *The Rebordering of North America*. New York: Routledge, 2003.

Bankston, Carl L., III, and Daniel Antoinette Hidalgo, eds. *Immigration in U.S. History*. Hackensack, N.J.: Salem Press, 2006.

Daniels, Roger. *Guarding the Golden Door: American Immigration Policy and Immigrants Since 1882*. New York: Hill and Wang, 2005.

Hayduk, Robert. *Democracy for All: Restoring Immigrant Voting Rights in the United States*. New York: Routledge, 2006.

Huntington, Samuel P. *Who Are We: The Challenges to America's Identity*. New York: Simon & Shuster, 2004.

Nevins, Joseph. *Operation Gatekeeper: The Rise of the Illegal Alien and the U.S.–Mexico Boundary*. New York: Routledge, 2002.

Ngai, Mae. *Impossible Subjects: Illegal Aliens and the Making of Modern America*. Princeton, N.J.: Princeton University Press, 2004.

Smith, Robert. *Mexican New York: Transnational Lives of New Immigrants*. Berkeley: University of California Press, 2006.

Yans-McLaughlin, Virginia, ed. *Immigration Reconsidered: History, Sociology, and Politics*. New York: Oxford University Press, 1990.

Zolberg, Asitide. *A Nation by Design: Immigration Policy in the Fashioning of America*. Cambridge, Mass.: Harvard University Press, 2006.

FURTHER READING

Allport, Allan. *Immigration Policy*. Philadelphia: Chelsea House Books, 2005.

Byers, Ann. *The History of U.S. Immigration: Coming to America*. Berkeley Heights, N.J.: Enslow, 2006.

DiConsiglio, John, ed. *Coming to America: Voices of Teenage Immigrants*. New York: Scholastic, 2002.

Hoobler, Dorothy, and Thomas Hoobler. *Scholastic History of Immigration*. New York: Scholastic Reference, 2003.

Lawlor, Veronica, ed. *I Was Dreaming to Come to America: Memories from the Ellis Island Oral History Project*. New York: Viking, 1995.

Martin, Michael. *Chinese Americans*. Philadelphia: Chelsea House Publishers, 2003.

Index

ABOUT THE AUTHOR

Jeannine Ouellette is the author of the children's picture book *Mama Moon*. She has published hundreds of essays and articles in national and regional magazines, and her work has been reproduced in several anthologies, including *Women's Lives: Multicultural Perspectives*. She is the recipient of first-place awards in writing and editing from the Medill School of Journalism and the winner of a 2006 Page One Award from the Society of Professional Journalists.

IMAGE CREDITS